DOGS TO THE RESCUE!

FIRE DOGS

By Sara Green

BELLWETHER MEDIA • MINNEAPOLIS, MN

Jump into the cockpit and take flight with Pilot books. Your journey will take you on high-energy adventures as you learn about all that is wild, weird, fascinating, and fun!

This edition first published in 2014 by Bellwether Media, Inc.

No part of this publication may be reproduced in whole or in part without written permission of the publisher. For information regarding permission, write to Bellwether Media, Inc., Attention: Permissions Department, 5357 Penn Avenue South, Minneapolis, MN 55419.

Library of Congress Cataloging-in-Publication Data

Green, Sara, 1964-
 Fire dogs / by Sara Green.
    pages cm. – (Pilot: Dogs to the rescue!)
 Includes bibliographical references and index.
 Summary: "Engaging images accompany information about fire dogs. The combination of high-interest subject matter and narrative text is intended for students in grades 3 through 7"–Provided by publisher.
 ISBN 978-1-60014-953-5 (hardcover : alk. paper)
 1. Detector dogs–Juvenile literature. 2. Arson investigation–Juvenile literature. 3. Fire investigation–Juvenile literature. I. Title.
 HV8079.A7G74 2014
 363.25'9642–dc23
                                          2013002379

Printed in the United States of America, North Mankato, MN.

TABLE OF CONTENTS

FIRE DOG AT THE SCENE

Several fire trucks race across town with their sirens blaring. An old, empty hotel is on fire. Will the firefighters arrive in time to put it out?

At the scene, they discover the fire is going strong. Flames leap from the hotel's windows, and soon the roof collapses. The firefighters work hard, but the hotel burns to the ground. Nobody knows how the fire started. It might have been an accident, but some suspect **arson**.

The next day, the police begin to investigate. They bring along Lila, a specially trained dog. Lila sniffs the burned **debris** of the hotel. Suddenly, she sits down next to a pile of ashes and stares at her **handler**. The police officers know that Lila has sniffed an **accelerant**. Now the police believe that someone probably started the fire on purpose.

SNIFFING OUT EVIDENCE

Fire dogs are highly trained canines that have helped firefighters and police officers for more than 25 years. They are officially called arson dogs or accelerant detection dogs. When there is a **suspicious** fire, fire investigators must decide if the fire was an accident or set on purpose. They search for **flammable** liquids called accelerants. **Arsonists** use these liquids to start fires. Common accelerants include gasoline, lighter fluid, and paint thinner.

Fire investigators often have a difficult time finding accelerants in debris. Many rely on dogs to assist in the search. With their sharp sense of smell, arson dogs can easily sniff out tiny amounts of accelerants. They can even sniff them through water, mud, and snow. The dogs cover ground more quickly than humans. They can find **evidence** of a crime much faster than people or machines.

The Test Dog

The Bureau of Alcohol, Tobacco, and Firearms (ATF) started training arson dogs in 1984. Their test dog was a yellow Lab named Nellie. Since then, the ATF has certified more than 100 arson dogs.

Labrador Retrievers and Lab mixes are the most common arson dogs. Other popular breeds are German Shepherds, Golden Retrievers, and Belgian Malinois. Arson dogs must be intelligent, curious, and good at **tracking**. They must be calm but also have enough energy to work long, stressful days.

Breeds of Fire Dogs

German Shepherd

Golden Retriever

Belgian Malinois

Profile: Labrador Retriever

Sense of Smell
The Lab can sniff out a drop of gasoline in wreckage the size of a suburban house.

Size
Height: 21 to 25 inches (53 to 64 centimeters)

Weight: 60 to 90 pounds (27 to 41 kilograms)

Intelligence
The Lab is the seventh smartest dog breed. The dog can learn new commands with little repetition and will obey them almost every time.

Most arson dogs come from rescue shelters. **Guide dog** schools also donate dogs to arson teams. Some of their dogs are intelligent and well behaved but get easily distracted by smells. This prevents them from being reliable guide dogs. However, this means they can be skilled fire investigators.

A DETECTIVE IN TRAINING

There are several arson dog training centers in the United States. One of largest is in Maine. An **insurance agency** provides money to train the dogs. The agency uses arson dogs to discover the cause of fires in homes and buildings. This saves the company thousands of dollars each year. Trained arson dogs work all over the country. Some are even sent to help investigators in Canada.

Most arson dogs live with their handlers. These people are usually police officers or firefighters who investigate fires. Handlers and their dogs form strong bonds of friendship. This helps them trust each other both on and off the job.

Lots of Sniffs
During training, many arson dogs sniff accelerants up to 125 times each day. This adds up to 45,000 sniffs each year.

Common Accelerants

- camp fuel
- charcoal lighter fluid
- diesel
- gasoline
- jet fuel
- lacquer thinner
- lamp oil
- kerosene
- paint thinner
- paint remover
- turpentine

Arson dog training lasts four or more weeks. First, dogs learn to sit where they smell gasoline. With their noses, they point to where the scent is the strongest. This is called a **passive response**. The dogs alert their handlers to a scent without damaging the scene. Food is their reward for sitting.

Next, dogs learn to find other accelerants. Handlers hide these liquids in cement cracks and on stairways. They put drops on towels and pieces of cotton. The dogs receive food rewards when they locate the accelerants. Finally, dogs learn to tell the difference between accelerants and other liquids that smell similar. A **chemist** checks if dogs correctly identified the accelerants. A perfect score leads to **certification**.

A DANGEROUS JOB

Arson dogs often work in dangerous conditions. They must navigate obstacles, such as fallen beams and broken glass. These objects can cut or injure dogs. Fire makes floors weak and can cause them to cave in. Dogs risk falling through holes. Accelerants can burn a dog's skin, eyes, and nose.

Handlers protect their dogs as best they can. They inspect a scene before allowing dogs to enter. They make sure burned areas are cooled down. Handlers also note the spots where dangers are the greatest. Many dogs wear booties to protect their paws. Some wear **reflective harnesses**. This helps their handlers see them in dark places. All handlers have canine first aid skills. If the dogs are injured, the handlers know how to care for them.

reflective harness

booties

15

Arson dogs investigate places other than burned houses and buildings. They search vehicles and areas near fire scenes. They also search people. These dogs can sniff accelerants on clothes and shoes. Many work in forests after a suspicious fire. They find a suspect's scent trail and follow it. Some even lead investigators to a suspect's front door!

Handlers sometimes bring their arson dogs to courtrooms. A handler describes the dog's training and experience to the judge. This helps convince the court that the dog's findings are valuable to the case.

Today, there are more than 200 arson dog teams
working in the United States. The dogs must pass
a test every year to keep their certification. They
must show that they can still sniff out accelerants
without mistakes.

Handlers also seek to improve their skills. Every year,
they take classes about dog health and safety. They
learn about the latest training techniques and study laws
about arson. This keeps the team ready and able to
solve crimes.

Arson dogs can work for up to 10 years. Once they
retire, they usually live at home with their handlers.
Sometimes new families adopt them. Wherever they
live, the dogs enjoy a well-deserved, restful retirement.

SADIE THE FIRE DOG

An arson dog named Sadie was a finalist for the 2011 American Humane Association Hero Dog Award. This national award is given to dogs that provide outstanding service to people. Sadie is a black Lab that lives in Colorado. She and her handler, Agent Jerry Means, work for the Colorado Bureau of Investigation.

Sadie and Agent Means have investigated hundreds of fires since 2007 and helped solve many cases. Sadie has never lost a case in court! She is also extremely friendly. Sadie does around 50 demonstrations each year with Agent Means. She helps children and adults learn about fire safety and prevention. Sadie is truly a hero to all who know her!

A Model Dog

Sadie is the model for the National Fire Dog Monument. This sculpture is located in Washington, D.C. It honors both firefighters and arson dogs.

21

GLOSSARY

accelerant—a liquid used to start and spread a fire quickly

arson—setting fire to physical property on purpose

arsonists—people who start fires on purpose

certification—the process that recognizes that a dog has mastered specific job skills

chemist—a scientist who studies chemicals and how they react

debris—scattered remains of something that has been destroyed

evidence—information that shows whether something is true or false

flammable—able to start on fire easily

guide dog—a dog that guides blind people

handler—a person who is responsible for a highly trained dog

insurance agency—an office that pays for damages caused by events such as fires, floods, and storms

passive response—a calm, quiet reaction; sitting still and staring is a passive response.

reflective harnesses—special harnesses that reflect light to help handlers see their dogs in dark places; a harness is a strap that fits around a dog's shoulders and chest.

retire—to stop working

suspicious—something that appears to be wrong

tracking—following scent trails

TO LEARN MORE

AT THE LIBRARY

Bozzo, Linda. *Fire Dog Heroes*. Berkeley Heights, N.J.: Bailey Books/Enslow Publishers, 2011.

Latham, Donna. *Fire Dogs*. New York, N.Y.: Bearport Pub., 2006.

Meyer, Karl. *Dog Heroes: A Story Poster Book*. North Adams, Mass.: Storey Publishing, 2008.

ON THE WEB

Learning more about fire dogs is as easy as 1, 2, 3.

1. Go to www.factsurfer.com.

2. Enter "fire dogs" into the search box.

3. Click the "Surf" button and you will see a list of related Web sites.

With factsurfer.com, finding more information is just a click away.

INDEX